My Memories was designed as a journal. Place your own photo in the pocket and write down your feelings and memories of that special person or occasion. Keep it as a keepsake for yourself or give it as a gift.